An Adult Story Book

SHUT THE F*CK UP OR ELSE YOU'LL GET FIRED!

CRISTINA CARBALLO-PERELMAN, M.D.

**SHUT THE F*CK UP
OR ELSE YOU'LL GET FIRED!**
An Adult Story Book
by Cristina Carballo-Perelman, M.D.

Cover Design and Illustrations by: Swapan Debnath

Library of Congress Control Number 2015914894
ISBN: 978-0-9967412-4-8

You've finally scored the job you so wanted,

But you don't understand why your new colleagues are daunted.

You ask every day, but the only clear answer is,

"Shut the fuck up, or else you'll get fired!

You try to be honest about how things are done.

You even ask questions to learn more from,

But all you get back every time you ask questions is,

"Shut the fuck up, or else you'll get fired!

You start getting stressed; you don't want to falter,

You want to achieve and climb even higher,

Every time that you think you have climbed
another step,

All you are told is,

"Shut the fuck up, or else you'll get fired!

You know that you are learning and need to teach others,

But others don't listen and don't have any druthers.

You tell them, "Please listen, I want to say something",

But all you get back is,

"Shut the fuck up, or else you'll get fired!

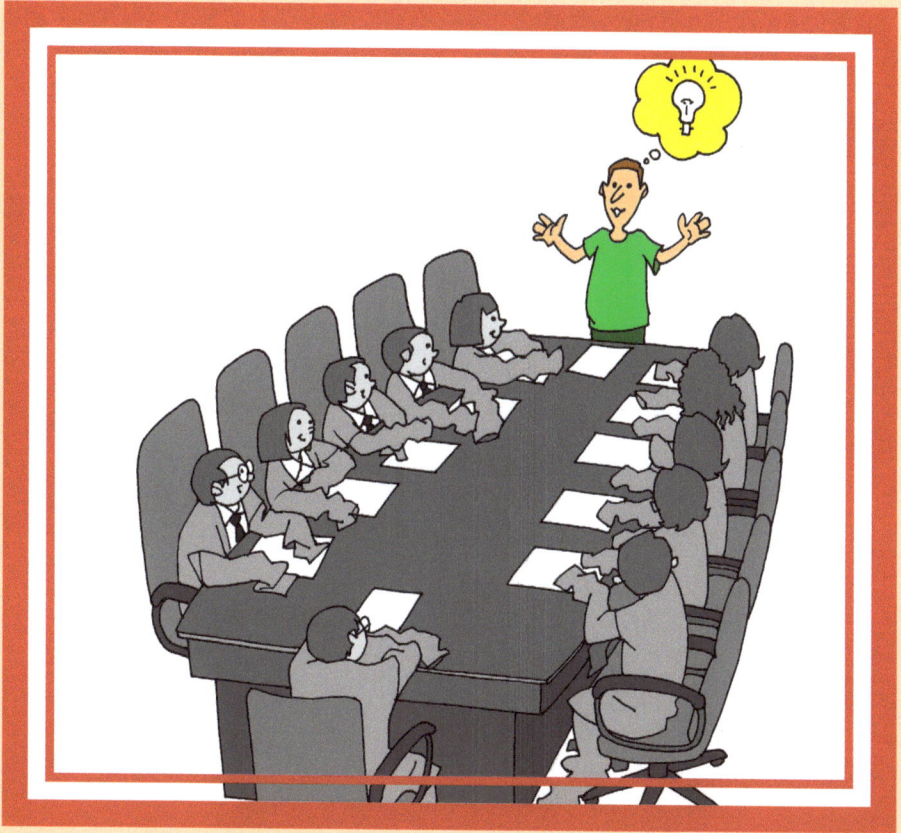

You trust your own instincts and try to trust others,

But neither is able to work with the other.

You hem and you haw and try to look forward,

But all you can see are the lies, which are less than straightforward.

When you ask and you search to find truth in the matter,

All you are told is,

"Shut the fuck up, or else you'll get fired!

You try to stay humble and speak very little,

You listen and learn but feel very brittle.

The others see humble as being a wimp,

And you try to tell them it's better to skimp

On being arrogant and full of yourself,

But all you are told is,

"Shut the fuck up, or else you'll get fired!

You tell them, "C'mon, lets have some respect for

me and the others",

But all you get back is, "Respect is too highly rated

to even bother."

You think and you ponder, "Oh what can I do?

So you try one more time to show them what to do,

After all, it's only with respect,

That others respect you, but all you get back is,

"Shut the fuck up, or else you'll get fired!

So you try another way, to work as a team,

To show them together as one, will be a dream!

When you try this last time, they all look at you and laugh,

"Don't you realize, you fool, that you have lots of sass.

To be truthful to you, you have nothing to say,

Your ideas are nil,

Your thoughts are just ok.

You might want to work as a team with respect, you might want to be honest, but that's not ok.

Because if you want to climb higher and make a big dent, you better,

"Shut the fuck up, or else you'll get fired!

So that is my story, a sad one that's true.

All I ever wanted was what I could never do.

I wanted to be honest and trust all the others,

I wanted to learn so I could go farther,

I wanted to achieve and show them the way.

I tried to show humility, but that was not ok.

And respect just was laughed at and made me feel foolish,

And lastly the teamwork was only called ghoulish.

And so I tell you this story so you can learn,   that if you start working and face this in turn,

Run, run, fast away and leave, before you are told,

"Shut the fuck up, or else you'll get fired!

So my last words to you,

are that if you never want to hear,

"Shut the fuck up, or else you'll get fired!

Then stay true to the person you really are,

**"And always remember
you will again, get hired!**

About the Author

Cristina Carballo-Perelman, M.D., has been a neonatologist for twenty seven years. Although she stayed true to her ethics and her professional dedication, she was fired. In this humorous book, the author pokes fun at a traumatic event to help the reader understand that they too will survive.

This book is a great accompaniment to Fired: Challenging the Status Quo and the Aftermath, which describes in detail the type of company or corporation where an employee might be most successful in, the qualities needed to thrive in today's work environment without losing one's soul and the grieving process necessary to survive if indeed you were fired. The author lives in Scottsdale, Arizona, with her husband and her two dogs and one cat. Her daughter, who just finished her B.S. in Biology, is presently pursuing a career in healthcare.

www.ingramcontent.com/pod-product-compliance
Lightning Source LLC
Chambersburg PA
CBHW041816240326
41458CB00159BA/6464